WEB MIRAGE: DECODING THE HISTORY OF ONLINE DECEPTION

Contents

I. Presentation

The web, hailed as one of the best accomplishments of the advanced period, has changed the manner in which we impart, access data, and lead our regular routines. Notwithstanding, hiding underneath the outer layer of this huge computerized scene is a shadowy domain of trickery and misrepresentations that have developed with the actual medium. The history of fake things on the internet is a complicated story that intertwines with the very fabric of our online existence. It spans from the early days of harmless pranks to the sophisticated world of deep fakes and cyber threats.

A. Definition and Advancement of Phony Things

The expression "counterfeit things" includes a wide cluster of tricky substance that ranges from harmless tricks to malevolent falsehood crusades. At first, the web was a jungle gym for innocuous tricks and metropolitan legends, frequently shared through networking messages or release sheets. As the advanced scene developed, so did the refinement of tricky works on, leading to additional intricate and significant types of deception.

The development of phony things on the web is intently attached to mechanical headways. In the early days of the World Wide Web, what started out as simple pranks and hoaxes has evolved into a multifaceted problem that includes deep fakes, online scams, fake news, and cyber threats. The multiplication of web-based entertainment stages and the simplicity with which data spreads online have amplified the effect of misleading works on, representing a huge danger to the uprightness of data and the trust clients place in web-based content.

B. The Inescapability of Misdirection On the web

Double dealing on the web isn't restricted to a particular corner of the web; It is everywhere in digital media. Content that is misleading has spread to news websites, email inboxes, social media platforms, and even personal communication channels. The reliability of information and users' ability to distinguish between truth and fiction are seriously compromised by the prevalence of deception.

The quick scattering of data on the web has established a climate where falsehood can become a web sensation in no time, affecting popular assessment, molding political stories, and in any event, influencing monetary business sectors. The inescapability of trickery online isn't just a mechanical test yet in addition a cultural one, requesting an aggregate work to address and relieve its ramifications.

As we leave on this investigation of the historical backdrop of phony things on the web, perceiving the unique idea of this phenomenon is fundamental. From the beginning of the web to the present, the scene of trickery has consistently advanced, driven by mechanical development, cultural changes, and the versatility of the individuals who try to take advantage of the weaknesses of online stages.

In the accompanying segments, we will dive into the various ages of online trickiness, analyzing the key achievements, difficulties, and suggestions related with each stage. From the energetic tricks of the past to the modern controls of the present, the historical backdrop of phony things on the web is an arresting story that reveals insight into the more obscure parts of our interconnected computerized world.

II. Early Days: Pre-Web Tricks

A. Tricks and Metropolitan Legends

The beginning of the web were set apart by a feeling of oddity and trial and error, as clients investigated the huge capability of this arising innovation. During this period, the idea of phony substance essentially rotated around innocuous tricks and metropolitan legends that tracked down another mechanism for dispersal. The jovial nature of early internet deception was exemplified by chain letters that were sent through email inboxes and frequently stated that they would bring good fortune or terrible consequences.

Tricks were predominant in web-based discussions and discussion boards, where clients participated in exercises that went from making imaginary characters to creating elaborate stories intended to delude and entertain. These tricks, while frequently guiltless and entertaining, laid the basis for the more refined types of misdirection that would arise in the years to come.

The spread of metropolitan legends, frequently introduced as wake up calls or stunning stories, turned into a typical event. These accounts went after the naivety of early web clients, utilizing the curiosity of the internet based space to enhance their effect. While the goal behind these deceptions was frequently harmless, they set up for the more evil and powerful types of falsehood that would later arise.

B. Junk Letters and Email Scams

In the beginning of the web, email arose as an essential method of correspondence, and with it came the expansion of networking letters and email deceptions. Clients got messages guaranteeing that sending the email to a specific number of beneficiaries would bring them karma or forestall some looming calamity. These advanced junk letters took advantage of the interconnected idea of the web, spreading quickly and generally.

Email lies, frequently taking on the appearance of pressing admonitions or electrifying news, planned to beguile beneficiaries into making explicit moves. Whether it was spreading bogus wellbeing data, cautioning of non-existent PC infections, or advancing unwarranted paranoid notions, these deceptions gained by the trust that clients set in the beginning web-based climate.

While these early types of trickery were generally innocuous, they laid the preparation for the development of additional modern and malevolent practices. The methods used by those attempting to manipulate and deceive users evolved with the internet, paving the way for subsequent chapters in the history of fake things on the internet.

In the ensuing segments, we will investigate how the scene of online trickery developed with the appearance of virtual entertainment, leading to additional effective and unavoidable types of phony substance. A significant turning point occurred when innocent pranks and urban legends gave way to the era of social media deception, laying the groundwork for the difficulties we face in distinguishing fact from fiction in the digital age.

III. The Introduction of Virtual Entertainment Duplicity

A. Ascent of Phony Profiles

As the web progressed into the period of virtual entertainment, the scene of trickiness went through a significant change. Web-based entertainment stages gave rich ground to the multiplication of phony profiles, making a favorable place for people to expect misleading personalities and control online collaborations. From harmless social experimentation to more sinister goals like cyberbullying, propagandizing, or engaging in online scams, the reasons behind creating fake profiles varied.

The straightforwardness with which clients could make profiles on stages like Facebook, Twitter, and Instagram permitted tricky entertainers to lay out a presence, frequently imitating genuine people or manufacturing completely imaginary people. These phony profiles were not restricted to people; organizations, associations, and even state run administrations before long perceived the capability of utilizing counterfeit personas to propel their plans or control public insight.

The ascent of phony profiles acquainted another aspect with online trickiness, taking advantage of the trust intrinsic in friendly associations. Companions, family, and partners could unwittingly draw in with false records, prompting the spread of deception and disarray. Online entertainment stages, at first intended to cultivate certified associations, ended up wrestling with the test of recognizing valid and misleading clients.

B. Fabricated Stories and Viral Hoaxes

Social media's capacity for rapid information dissemination made it a potent instrument for the propagation of viral hoaxes and fabricated stories. With the snap of a button, a bogus story could arrive at a large number of clients, molding general assessment and impacting true occasions. Misleading entertainers immediately jumping all over this chance, making and spreading content intended to bring out close to home reactions and take advantage of the calculations that represented substance deceivability.

The development of phony news sites, intended to mirror genuine news sources, added one more layer to the trickiness. These sites distributed electrifying and frequently altogether made up stories, benefiting from the viral idea of online entertainment sharing. These stories were frequently consumed by users who were accustomed to the fast-paced and scroll-heavy nature of their social media feeds without critically evaluating their credibility, which further fueled the spread of false information.

Viral lies, portrayed by electrifying cases or doctored pictures, turned into a typical event. From misleading VIP passing's to manufactured logical forward leaps, the web turned into a favorable place for melodrama. The close to home effect of these scams frequently eclipsed objective examination, prompting the boundless acknowledgment of misleading stories and adding to the disintegration of confidence in web-based data.

As online entertainment double dealing kept on advancing, it laid the basis for additional complex types of control, including the approach of deep fakes and the weaponization of deception for political purposes. The inception of deceptive content on social media was a turning point in the history of fake content on the internet, highlighting the need for novel strategies to deal with the problems posed by deceptive content in the digital age.

In the resulting areas, we will investigate the movement of online duplicity into the domains of phony news, deep fakes, and network protection dangers, unwinding the mind boggling woven artwork of falsehood that keeps on molding our web-based encounters.

IV. Counterfeit News and Deception

A. Development of Phony News Sites

The expansion of phony news addresses a huge achievement in the development of online trickery. Counterfeit news sites, intended to impersonate real news sources, arose as a powerful weapon in the dispersal of deception. These locales took on proficient looking formats, convincing titles, and manufactured stories that frequently played on the feelings and inclinations of the crowd.

The essential inspiration driving making counterfeit news was not simply entertainment or innocuous tricking; it turned into a device for political control, misleading content income, and philosophical fighting. No sweat of distributing on the web, misleading entertainers took advantage of the public's confidence in media sources, planting disarray and dissolving the believability of real reporting.

The effect of phony news was not restricted to the virtual domain; it gushed out over into this present reality, affecting general assessment, influencing decisions, and adding to social polarization. The speed at which deception could spread via virtual entertainment stages exacerbated the test, making it challenging for reality checkers and stages to balance the viral scattering of misleading accounts.

B. Influence on Open Insight and Political Scene

Counterfeit news employed a strong impact on open discernment and the political scene. In different occurrences, created stories designated explicit people, political figures, or minimized gatherings, enhancing existing divisions inside society. Deceptive actors used echo chambers and confirmation biases to influence public sentiment, revealing the weaponization of misinformation for political gain.

Races all over the planet became landmarks for disinformation crusades. Bogus stories, decisively coordinated discharges, and the utilization of web-based entertainment as a misleading publicity instrument showed the way that phony news could shape political talk and impact elector conduct. The repercussions of such control were not restricted to the virtual domain, as they substantially affected the vote based process and the soundness of countries.

The battle to battle counterfeit news brought about reality actually taking a look at drives and expanded investigation of online substance. Online entertainment stages confronted mounting strain to resolve the issue, prompting the execution of calculations and arrangements pointed toward recognizing and alleviating the effect of bogus data. However, ongoing innovation in the fight against misinformation is required due to the dynamic nature of online deception, which continually posed a challenge to these efforts.

As we explore the complicated snare of phony news and falsehood, perceiving the more extensive ramifications of these misleading practices on the texture of our societies is fundamental. The weaponization of data, energized by the fast scattering capacities of the web, has tried the strength of popularity based organizations as well as featured the requirement for aggregate liability in cultivating a reliable computerized climate.

In the resulting segments, we will investigate the development of online duplicity into the domain of deep fakes, investigating the mechanical progressions that have additionally obscured the line among the real world and fiction in the computerized age. The difficulties presented by counterfeit news and falsehood act as a forerunner to the more intricate and nuanced types of duplicity that keep on forming our web-based encounters.

V. Deepfakes and Controlled Media

A. Prologue to Deepfakes

The coming of deepfakes denoted a turning point throughout the entire existence of online misdirection, presenting a degree of complexity that obscured the line among the real world and fiction. Deepfakes, controlled by computerized reasoning (artificial intelligence) and profound learning calculations, empower the consistent control of sound and video content, permitting people to superimpose faces onto various bodies or even manufacture altogether sensible yet fictitious situations.

The expression "deepfake" itself is gotten from "profound learning" and "phony," accentuating the utilization of profound brain organizations to make exceptionally persuading controlled media. At first, deepfakes arose as a type of diversion, with lovers trading faces in film scenes or superimposing superstars into entertaining recordings. Nonetheless, the innovation immediately took a hazier turn as it turned into a device for pernicious plan, going from vengeance pornography to political publicity.

B. Implications for Trust and Authenticity

In today's digital world, the rise of deepfakes has significant repercussions for trust and authenticity. The capacity to control varying media happy with such accuracy challenges customary techniques for checking the veracity of media. In a time where seeing is never again fundamentally accepting, the actual groundworks of truth and confidence in the computerized domain are raised doubt about.

Deepfakes have been taken advantage of for different odious purposes, including spreading falsehood, creating compromising substance, and in any event, imitating people of note. Policymakers, tech companies, and the general public have expressed concern due to the possibility that these manipulated media could cause panic, harm reputations, or sway public opinion.

Virtual entertainment stages, perceiving the danger presented by deepfakes, have carried out measures to identify and eliminate such happy. In any case, the wait-and-see game between deepfake makers and content balance calculations endures, highlighting the continuous difficulties in tending to this type of misdirection successfully.

The effect of deepfakes stretches out past the advanced domain, saturating certifiable results. Political figures might end up at the focal point of controlled outrages, and people might become survivors of fraud through the formation of reasonable however altogether fictitious recordings. The mental cost for those designated by deepfake content raises moral worries, underscoring the requirement for a complete way to deal with moderate the possible damages.

As innovation keeps on progressing, so too will the abilities of deep fake innovation. The ever-evolving nature of online deception is exemplified by the arms race between those who create manipulated content and those who seek to detect and counter it. We will look at the prevalence of online scams, cyber threats, and the broader effects of technological advancements on the internet's landscape of fake goods in the following sections. The time of deep fakes fills in as a wake up call, encouraging us to stay watchful even with progressively modern types of computerized control.

VI. Online Tricks and Cheats

A. Phishing Plans

The ascent of online tricks and cheats addresses a dim underside of the web, where misleading entertainers exploit the trust and weaknesses of clients for monetary profit. Among the most inescapable types of online duplicity are phishing plans. Phishing includes the utilization of false strategies to fool people into unveiling delicate data, for example, usernames, passwords, or monetary subtleties.

Phishing assaults frequently appear as misleading messages, messages, or sites intended to emulate real elements. These interchanges normally mimic confided in foundations, like banks, web-based entertainment stages, or government offices, making a misguided feeling of direness to provoke casualties into uncovering secret data. Phishing schemes rely on social engineering techniques that take advantage of trust and human psychology.

As innovation advances, so do phishing methods. Progressed phishing assaults might consolidate customized subtleties got from information breaks, causing the tricky messages to show up really persuading. The continuous wait-and-see game among cybercriminals and network safety estimates highlights the requirement for steady watchfulness despite these internet based tricks.

B. Venture and Sentiment Tricks

Past phishing, online tricks envelop a more extensive range, including speculation tricks and sentiment tricks. In speculation tricks, fraudsters draw people with commitments of rewarding profits from ventures, frequently utilizing complex sites and convincing correspondence to make a deception of authenticity. Casualties may accidentally move assets to fake records, bringing about monetary misfortunes.

Sentiment tricks include building counterfeit heartfelt connections to take advantage of people sincerely and monetarily. Con artists, frequently working under bogus personalities, lay out web-based associations with clueless casualties, acquiring their trust prior to creating elaborate stories to demand cash. These tricks go after the weakness and generosity of people looking for friendship, leaving casualties shattered as well as monetarily crushed.

The pervasiveness of these tricks features the flexibility of misleading entertainers in taking advantage of developing web-based ways of behaving. As individuals progressively take part in web-based exercises, from monetary exchanges to social connections, the possible focuses for tricks duplicate. A multifaceted strategy that incorporates public education, technological safeguards, and legal measures is required to combat online scams.

The outcomes of succumbing to online tricks reach out past

monetary misfortunes. People might encounter close to home misery, harmed notorieties, and a deficiency of confidence in web-based connections. The ever-evolving strategies of fraudsters necessitate constant adaptation in order to counteract their schemes, but law enforcement agencies and cyber security professionals continue to work to dismantle scam networks.

In the resulting segments, we will dive into the domain of network safety dangers and computerized wholesale fraud, looking at how the interconnected idea of the web has led to a perplexing scene of online dangers. The history of online scams and frauds serves as a stark reminder of how important it is to be educated and vigilant when navigating the digital landscape, where deceptive actors continue to exploit the unsuspecting for illicit gains.

VII. A. Hacking Incidents

There are a plethora of cyber security threats as a result of the increasing reliance on digital infrastructure and the proliferation of interconnected systems. Hacking episodes, going from individual information breaks to enormous scope digital assaults, have turned into an inescapable and modern type of online trickery.

Cybercriminals, furnished with cutting edge apparatuses and procedures, exploit weaknesses in programming, organizations, and gadgets to acquire unapproved admittance to delicate data. Information breaks, where enormous volumes of individual or corporate information are compromised, have become alarmingly normal. Prominent episodes, for example, the Equifax break, highlight the expansive results of hacking on people and associations the same.

There are many different reasons for hacking incidents. Hoodlums might look for monetary benefit through the offer of taken information on the dull web, participate in corporate secret activities, or seek after philosophical objectives by upsetting basic foundation. The consistently developing nature of digital dangers requires ceaseless progressions in network safety measures to shield against unapproved access and information breaks.

B. Taken Individual Data

Computerized fraud, a result of hacking and other tricky practices, includes the unapproved securing and utilization of a singular's very own data for false purposes. This can incorporate taking Government managed retirement numbers, charge card subtleties, or login certifications

The results of computerized fraud stretch out past monetary misfortunes. Casualties might encounter harm shockingly scores, lawful difficulties coming about because of fake exercises led in their name, and the burdensome course of recovering their taken character. The interconnected idea of online stages and the immense measures of individual data put away carefully establish a climate ready for double-dealing by cybercriminals.

Because of the developing danger of computerized fraud, people and associations have expanded their emphasis on network protection measures. Multifaceted confirmation, encryption, and ordinary security reviews are among the techniques utilized to safeguard delicate data. Also, public mindfulness crusades expect to instruct clients about the dangers of sharing individual data on the web and the significance of rehearsing great digital cleanliness.

The fight against online protection dangers is a continuous test, with cybercriminals persistently adjusting their strategies to take advantage of new weaknesses.

Coordinated effort between legislatures, organizations, and people is essential to creating vigorous network protection systems and answering actually to arising dangers. As we explore the intricacies of the computerized age, the historical backdrop of hacking episodes and advanced data fraud highlights the basic of focusing on network safety to guarantee the respectability of our internet based connections and safeguard against vindictive entertainers looking to take advantage of weaknesses for their benefit.

VIII. The Waiting Game: Battling On the web Trickery

A. Truth Really looking at Drives

The raising danger of online trickery has incited the improvement of reality checking drives pointed toward confirming the precision of data circling on the web. Truth checkers, frequently autonomous associations or news sources, investigate cases, proclamations, and news stories to decide their legitimacy. By utilizing thorough analytical techniques, truth checkers assume a significant part in exposing misleading data and advancing straightforwardness.

Traditional media outlets are not the only ones where

misinformation is spread; it saturates web-based entertainment stages and online gatherings. Reality checking associations team up with tech organizations to carry out instruments that recognize and signal possibly bogus substance. In recognition of their responsibility to combat deception, social media platforms have integrated fact-checking mechanisms to inform users about the veracity of shared information.

B. Lawful Reactions and Guidelines

State run administrations overall have answered the difficulties presented by online misdirection by authorizing lawful measures and guidelines. In some nations, laws against the dissemination of false information and fake news have been enacted. Those who are found guilty of intentionally disseminating false information face penalties. Be that as it may, adjusting the need to address misdirection with safeguarding opportunity of articulation stays a fragile test.

Regulations requiring tech companies to be held accountable for the content they publish on their platforms have also been formulated as a result of increased scrutiny. Regulation resolving issues like information protection, content control, and the spread of falsehood has been presented in different purviews. Finding some kind of harmony between protecting a free and open web and controling tricky practices requires continuous regulative endeavors and worldwide collaboration.

C. Moral Utilization of Innovation

As innovation keeps on progressing, moral contemplations assume a vital part in molding the turn of events and sending of computerized devices.
Mindfulness crusades and instructive drives intend to engage clients to basically assess online substance, perceive likely control, and recognize among dependable and tricky data.

The wait-and-see game between those making misleading substance and those attempting to neutralize it features the unique idea of online duplicity. To stay ahead of evolving deceptive practices, governments, technology companies, civil society, and individuals must work together as technological advancements bring both opportunities and challenges.

We will examine notable case studies, including well-known internet hoaxes and significant instances of fake news, in the following sections. These models give experiences into the fluctuated inspirations driving web-based double dealing and the colossal results it can have on people, social orders, and the computerized scene in general. The wait-and-see game keeps, encouraging us to stay cautious and proactive in the continuous fight against online trickiness.

XIV. Conclusion

A tapestry of innovation, deception, and societal transformation runs through the history of fake internet products. From the beginning of innocuous tricks and metropolitan legends to the complex scene of deep fakes, online double dealing has developed close by mechanical progressions, molding the manner in which we see and connect with advanced data.

The mental effect of web misdirection is apparent in the disintegration of trust and the mental consequences for clients. Trust, when a foundation of online communications, has been tested by the expansion of deception, counterfeit news, and manipulative practices. The mental predispositions exacerbated by online trickiness further confound the undertaking of knowing truth from fiction in the advanced age.

Innovation, a situation with two sides in the domain of online duplicity, both empowers and counters tricky practices. Mechanization and man-made brainpower have led to refined bots, deepfakes, and simulated intelligence created content, presenting new difficulties for content control and network safety. The waiting game between deceptive entertainers and those fighting internet based trickery highlights the powerful idea of this advancing scene.

Moral contemplations assume a critical part in exploring the intricacies of online double dealing.

Content makers, innovation engineers, and policymakers should focus on straightforwardness, client protection, and algorithmic decency to construct a computerized climate grounded in trust and credibility. Individuals are empowered to evaluate online content critically through educational initiatives and responsible technology use, both of which contribute to a more resilient online community.

As we expect future patterns and difficulties, the scene of online duplicity will probably keep on developing. The ascent of deepfake innovation, man-made intelligence driven double dealing methodologies, and the continuous weapons contest in network protection present complex difficulties that request creative arrangements. Fortifying moral norms, establishing vigorous guidelines, and encouraging a culture of mindful computerized citizenship will be fundamental in forming a future where the web is a dependable and solid wellspring of data.

All in all, the set of experiences and fate of phony things on the web are complicatedly connected to our decisions as people, the strategies we execute as social orders, and the advances we create as a worldwide local area. By embracing moral contemplations, mechanical development, and a promise to truth, we can explore the powerful scene of online duplicity and develop a computerized space that cultivates real associations, informed independent direction, and a common obligation to the quest for information.